T3-BNL-100

HEART INTO SOIL

Xue Di

HEART INTO SOIL

selected poems

translated by Keith Waldrop
with Wang Ping
Iona Crook
Janet Tan
and Hil Anderson

Burning Deck/Lost Roads
Providence/Barrington
1998

Acknowledgements

Some of these translations were first published in *Cathay, Manoa, Mid-American Review, Moonrabbit Review, The Asian Pacific Journal, The Providence Journal, The Temple, The World, Tyuonyi;* and in the anthologies, *This Same Sky,* ed. Naomi Shihab Nye (Four Winds Press) and *Contemporary Chinese Poetry,* ed. Wang Ping (Hanging Loose Press).

Flames was published as a chapbook by Paradigm Press (Providence, 1995).

Publication of the present Selected Poems was, in part, supported by a grant from the International Academy for Scholarship and the Arts through Bard College, Annandale-on-Hudson, and by donations from Burning Deck's angels: Leonard Brink, Steve Evans and Patrick O'Shea.

Burning Deck is the literature program of Anyart: Contemporary Arts Center, a tax-exempt non-profit corporation.

Cover design by Keith Waldrop
Cover photo by John Foraste

CONTENTS

Translator's note   7

I

poems written in China

	[translated by:]	
Starvation	[IC & KW]	11
Cloud	[IC & KW]	12
Another Kind of Tenderness	[IC & KW]	13
My Home	[WP & KW]	14
The Town Drunk	[WP & KW]	15
The Mushroom River	[WP & KW]	19

FLAMES:
Road	[WP & KW]	20
The Burning Silk Veil	[IC & KW]	21
Sower	[IC & KW]	23
The Gleaner	[WP & KW]	24
Poppy Fields	[WP & KW]	25
The Field Covered with Crows	[WP & KW]	26
Church	[WP & KW]	28
Injured Portrait	[IC & KW]	29
White Chinese Roses	[WP & KW]	31
Drawbridge	[WP & KW]	32
Scene	[WP & KW]	33
Sunflower	[WP & KW]	34
Tonight	[WP & KW]	36
Starry Night	[WP & KW]	37
Portrait	[WP & KW]	38
Blues	[WP & KW]	39

| Remembering | [IC & KW] | 41 |

II

poems written in America

First Love	[WP & KW]	47
Sitting in the Sun	[WP & KW]	48
Dream	[WP & KW]	39
Interplay	[WP & KW]	50
Zone	[WP & KW]	51
Respect	[WP & KW]	53
Homing	[WP & KW]	54
The Young Believer	[WP & KW]	56
Back	[WP & KW]	58
Earth	[WP & KW]	60
Drug	[WP & KW]	62
White Rubber Mask	[WP & KW]	64
Forgive	[WP & KW]	66
Faces	[JT & KW]	68
A Snake With Experience	[JT & KW]	69
The Shame of Flesh	[WP & KW]	70
Biography	[WP & KW]	72
Nocturne on a New Theme	[WP & KW]	74
Steps in the Dark	[WP & KW]	75
Hesitating Man	[WP & KW]	76
Anniversary	[WP & KW]	77
Crossed Realities	[WP & KW]	78
The Passage to Heaven	[WP & KW]	79
Turn Inward, Inward	[WP & KW]	80
Love	[WP & KW]	82
Love in Difficulty	[WP & KW]	84
March	[WP & KW]	86
The Skin of Love	[WP & KW]	88
Rainy Day	[WP & KW]	90
Nostalgia	[WP & KW]	91
Before the Good Weather	[HA & KW]	92

Translator's Note

Xue Di is a native of Beijing. After taking part in the 1989 demonstrations in Tian'anmen Square, he left China and, since 1990, has been a fellow in Brown University's Freedom to Write program. He has published two books of poems in Chinese, contributed to many magazines, and is also known as anthologist and critic.

This selection presents the poems in chronological order, those written before coming to the United States in part I and those written since in part II.

The English translations were done in two steps. First versions were prepared by people who know Chinese (the majority by Wang Ping) and from these, in consultation with the poet, I made final versions .

KW

I

STARVATION

I hear it, the howl of hunger
day and night frantic in my face
my own hands clawing in my throat
nails scarring the days as I throw them up

Tormented by others abandoned elsewhere
who tear my memories to shreds
I hear them sing
hauling my wounds up out of
time—dense sea of pain—my
four limbs quiet

The greatest wound
grows between my teeth
I hear that source of sound
I hear in my face the long dead
sing triumph and then sing it again
I thrust my hands into my throat
forcing a still channel screaming out

CLOUD

You are a beautiful cut-out
You are a bell at dusk
Tolling our body
Blood the past has collected
Returning by way of pain

You are childhood
One step the solitary takes into the night
Imbibing water's lyrical surface
You are that bright red mouth
Breathing our deep sigh in

You are a water jar
Standing against the sky
Mirroring by the road
Our broken pot-like face
Which severs, crying
Inwardly your quietness

ANOTHER KIND OF TENDERNESS

And now I wait
Your gentleness spawned me in a blade of grass
Your voice cuts through the dust
In the hollow of time your
lips have stung me with their music

And now I wait
Your hand reaches towards me like a river running
My mother, long departed, on the other shore
counts stones that glisten washed by the sky
Yes, another kind of tenderness

My life deprived of your soft skin
with five steel prongs I poke
holes in time's daylight
and out come my pure hunger, my pure
thirst, along with seven deep blue stars
And now I wait
One sentence from you made my desire blossom
and filled all my utterance
with tenderness

MY HOME

My home brings grapes to harvest
A warm afternoon my
wife, like a tender red fox
reaches her slender hand
into my chest, full of music

The windows are acrawl with bees
Flowers bloom in every word
My wife bustles, dressed in red, bangs the
screendoor in the bright sunshine...

I sit in a bronze chair
listening to roots roar away in the garden
and a drop of water seeping into a rock
A bird, far
off in my thought
                    cries

THE TOWN DRUNK

Soft night presses down on me
I hear the sad horn of the setting sun
It wiped the day's bronze mouth and
entered memory's dark cave
There's a wise man
thrusts water from him
I recognize the smell

How can a wolf survive the city
scratches himself against the stairs
crowds himself into the crowd
leg stained with wild berries. His
nose frozen, like a man's feet sticking
out from under the blanket
The sun's head is scarlet. Glass
cuts through his limbs like water
In dead of night I hear the howl
of dreamers on the run

My face
is woven like a bamboo basket
Soft night nestles me gently
The dark along my throat enters
the heart. In the wine's bright light
    I hear
his murmur and my murmur back
feel his hand
etching its loneliness
in the silver liquid. From memory's lair
a golden trumpet sounds

A buxom woman
draws all happiness
into her bright breasts
In the holy valley, covered with milkweed
you drive red foxes
I douse my flesh
in the shadow of their eyes
A hand sweeps the river
into death's panorama
The light flashes and goes out, leaving
bloody stains behind. The heart of blood:
night stirs the brimming past

Hatred! A big garish bird
darts through my throat into the sky
    depositing in my
    life her rock-like eggs
Scorpions nest under stones
snakes bask in the momentary sun
spring and summer take turns
trying to break my bones
Autumn's in the distant song
in dreams. Bees
sting busy travelers' cheeks

Pain! Hatred! My
city built with hollow bricks
bears the imprint of burnt grass
    Glass reflects
    patterns of water
Humans live within
    filling the hollows
The buildings stand for sex organs

Look at that man: that
    beautiful hollow human
is machine-made
He holds the same grass
and has to ask about his own face
Teeth, white enamel
gnashes the language of the dead
That river looks like a day
squeezed between two
nights. Pain! Disgust!
At night, my
limbs, you
hear doomsday coming

Where, in the pure
liquid, is purity?
I still see empty darkness
like the ring my lover gave me at the wedding
My wine, holy music
    covers my rocky beach
    my small mole cricket
In the thick shiny moss
I still see
a face I can't get rid of
    Teeth glint
on the rim of my wine glass
The city nests in my hair, like a beast
listening to horror chew at me
the pure clear liquid entering my veins
Pain! Pain! Born with me. Singing
through the four seasons. Laughing
Ablaze
    Piercing the dark
    Loneliness

I grasp
pain in its reflection
Blood talks to life through cracked skin
Pure red flowers
    open into shells
They remind me of some gorgeous fish
motionless behind a rock
My heart sinks in the water
talking casually with the long dead
Oh no, you can't see! That darkness
changed my face. The sun's hand
pulls my hand under the night
lets me know that in every object
there's a perfect stone
lets me know my lover
is also grass. Under her feet
the insects, who live brief lives
chirp the four seasons through. Let my lips
touch glass-thin praise. Whenever you wake
you see something surprising. Press
close to it! with your brilliant pain

THE MUSHROOM RIVER

That river is filled with mushrooms
    Yes, mother. The river you soaked your hands in
    My past flows by. The child in his red jacket exposes the
    skin of daylight. He is picking mushrooms on the river, his
    basket full of smiles
    Do not enter the dark misery of the forest. Mother

come back to the fairy tales with me:
    grandma hides the wolf in your voice, baring the day's teeth
    It's getting dark again. Will my love get lost? Mother, my
    childhood is gone forever
    Your hands bring the sound of water brimming from my eyes
    Do not go the lonely path of old age. Mother

Mushrooms. Butterflies dance in your silver hair
    The light is on. I walk towards you, along the river. The
    wolf in the fairy tale will die too, and the child do riffs
    on its teeth to go with the beautiful sounds of the road
    Memory pushes up like no end of pale, floating mushrooms
    carrying off the last of your years
    Go back inside. Don't stand in pain, waiting for me
    Remember how my poems send signals. I'll bring you songs of
    the vast fields

I'll describe for you the mushroom river

FLAMES:

*Poems dedicated
to Vincent van Gogh*

ROAD
   [van Gogh: "Road with Cypresses," 1890]

The workers are coming. Their blurred faces
impress on me the hardship of creation
Locate the roots of things
My breath flows through those roots
as if the flames of my whole body
surged up a cypress standing tall

Like a road twisting in the soul's uncertainty
Pale shell. Crying of wheat unsown
The human "past" shrill in the moonlight
Seeds sleeping in despair. The "future"
a good horse. Where the road is
open, perfect necks break with the strain

Still the bones of the cypress spit flames
From each drop of resin a squatting beast
vaults into the night, roars out starry
stars. Night is his vibrating gong
His claws rake human faces

THE BURNING SILK VEIL
[van Gogh: "Wheatfield with Cypresses," 1889]

Pale yellow world, color of my
heart fallen to the ground
listening to the land's anger
as mountain peaks stamp their feet
winter encroaching step by step
The stones in my flesh, in my eyes
swirl in the burning veil
The sky, great flat-bottomed basin
traps a child. Dead flowers in poverty
Who is behind me, walking in wrath
dragging my life along
pushing me to the earth
exhausted, the fields around my body burning

Who is life's slave? Take
the veil—throw it into the pit of "living"
"Death" shivers among a tangle of roots
A land intimidated can only be poor
Wheat still grows. The stones, incapable of sprouting
sink into endless silence
Take autumn away. Who is it who
uses this world's language
conceives within bitter
strength, makes children, attacks
the sky, grins at mankind? Is it
you, poet, each stick of your
skeleton a monkey wrench in the way of the world

The silk veil burns at your throat
Fire spurts from the sockets of your eyes
Those grains of wheat, those delicate gold
tongues of flame—I want to hold them
Earth. Clouds. You've hurt me before

21

The land's predators hold you tight
In the same way that this sad face, stuck onto
art, takes on a life, I—like
the others—have profited nothing

SOWER
  [van Gogh: "Sower with Setting Sun," 1888]

When the soil wakes from its deep sleep
sun paints the field's edges, revealing
a mouse's footprint baked into its surface
Wild geese begin their game with summer
Take their eggs, place them
over the lizard's fragile burrow. Fields

bulge up. The horses have galloped off
Give the odor of their groin to the swaying
cradle of the moon. I sit
inside the daisy girl's long flute
and feel earth's burgeoning desires

And just at this moment, you come
striding out of the sun, long stride across the
lumpy earth. Joy's radiance
turns your whole body to the dark
Grains gnaw at you. The land bleeds
You hear fruits crack open in the sky

Thinker among cattle, human
tongue of steel, your body
pressed to the dirt. All winter
you clutch the seeds and when you
open your fist, I wake to spring
watching your golden wheatfields sprout in blood

What joy! A mental halo
glazes the growing field
Your coming is mankind's primal song
I follow a foal as it wanders the riverbank
grazing on fruit blown down in the dusk

THE GLEANER
  [van Gogh: "Peasant Woman Stooping," 1885]

Pure ox horn. Then cows curved over wooden buckets
Gold husks buried in mud.   The earth, nourishment
Men slaughtering no one for grain

Then the land was given. At harvest time
houses went up between fields of wheat
Babies in baskets crying like tumbling fruit

Then you, a simple peasant girl
Your basket, from which a hare drank
and eight baby rabbits singing in your eyes

Grain! The village where childhood lived
where birds flew glittering like gold
attaching themselves to the neat river's face

Peasant girl! Round arms of a crescent moon
and bent like a crescent. Show me
how your forebears turn to gold in the soil's gift

Your fingers gleam with brightness
Wheat like a shower of diamonds
Watching you move with pious step

Girl, this heart—my heart—how
can it keep from falling into despair
in the ray of sunlight, close and airless

POPPY FIELDS
  [van Gogh: "Field with Poppies," 1890]

Summer ripens across the land. Swallows
transport southern waters into the orchard
Pomegranates shine like foreheads full of thoughts
Our hosts lie supine in berries
staring at the poppy-covered sky

The little animals are quiet
left paws crossed over right
Quail bob-white in their jars. Horses
strike fire near the house of white pines

O my life, take a break now
hang hunger on the poppy's hook
Sniff fruit pits, squeeze a handful of soil
See the sharp flames on golden pears

Close your eyes. Summer
slips into your sleep. As you wake
hear flowers chatter in the basket of the field
See endless sunflowers burning
like a hundred horseheads spinning madly in the sun

THE FIELD COVERED WITH CROWS
[van Gogh: "Wheat Field with Crows," 1890]

Waves of yellow wheat cry in my throat
    I stand on the heights
Everything ripens! Seeds tremble in the storm
singing towards the death-house. Crows
messengers of the abyss, wings with the gleam
of lilies. I come. I walk
My loneliness is like crystal
Who listens to my voice in poverty
gives me his hand, sustaining me
My sadness is a mirror
glistening in obscure human faces

I give up art, renounce religion
I stand on the heights. Gazing at the past
is like staring down an abyss of animal lairs
like casting my whole life into a battle with beauty
The spear of fantasy tilts at my throat
The fields are ripe. In ominous presentiment
    crows, from my feet
soar up through my veins

O pure wheat
seven pair of silver forks stab into your pit
    The storm carries you back
    —far away, a bright nothing
    trembles in stone as far as eye can see
I come. I'm lost
outside the weakness of art. What
can undo the crime of humans who insult the soul

On the heights
—the gate of death trembles over autumn waters
The sky folds, like a compressed spring
My heart! Look again at the fields. Grasp them
as if grasping the maelstrom that swallows up
your love. Cry that you love
it is the peak of death
The loner grows fruit-bearing limbs
Cry! Cry, brother, towards the nothing, crows
circling over crops, cawing their
cry to mankind

CHURCH
  [van Gogh: "The Church at Auvers," 1890]

Sacred music unsounding
I stare at you
flowers, roots of the grass. A woman defaced
I stand before the true altar
listening ever for the voice of gods
Weeds everywhere
the neigh of pursuing horses
My life of devotion
ignorant of evil
At sight of the mute solemn stone
my heart begins to bleed

Teach us how to love
Facing earth's molesters
facing the furious dying father
He has cleft the place that oppressed him with darkness
Tell us! how can we unfurl into the day
the banner of joyous purple fir
Birds and we embrace
Buildings stand erect. Lionesses bless herbivores
Babies kick in the bellies of men
like rivers on a rampage dividing the land

Holy spring! In my blood there's
    an altar-stone onto which music descends
Worship! Soil, petals of glass
the pinnacle! There my heart
registers simple songs of the sky
All things on earth revive ten thousand times from death
Now, my heart, pray for them all

INJURED PORTRAIT
[van Gogh: "Self-Portrait with Bandaged Ear and Pipe," 1889]

When music deserts the human heart, when
squirrels leap into pine cones, when antelopes
frisk on the ocean floor
when leaf shrinks back to branch, refusing point blank
to fall
we will all be empty vessels, our
vague eyes anthills strung along
beams of light, insect eggsacs
cemented to the heart, mouths
reduced to maledictions against barnyard animals
Everything, everything enrages me: this
nation of wild beasts, falling into decline
And as for poetry: a
stick between the jaws to block my bite

My ear: a sky-blue gem
touched by the crying of bugs
—summer lives inside. Place for a badger
to warm his paws night long. O deep
blue flame. Blue gem. My grandmother's
hands gripping the cow's udders
my irritable father: behold
a village, stately, its lonely glow
lighting my forlorn heart

Swarm of locusts! your chomp
encompasses earth. The people
are deaf and dumb, their ears no better than
saucers tied together by a string through the skull
Crocodile! Crocodile! my loved one, blue
blue gem, my aching
aching heart. Lop it off! Light
Light barricades my head. The sun

29

suddenly drops, warming the creatures
prancing in my blood
O gem, kingfisher-blue, to whom
shall I give you? who will
take you? Only the unstopped ear
Whose heart will hear the sacred harmonies

WHITE CHINESE ROSES
[van Gogh: "White Roses," 1890]

Flowers bloom in the house. Milk
shines on leaves. Amid a
cry of nightingales
my wife holds out the corolla of her hands
Rose! Chinese rose! Tell me
when did I lose
my peace

Cotton crosses the surface of the vase
Lambs gambol on tree tops. My daughter
lies among the bush's roots
Her nails, sharp thorns from the
dark, make my heart howl in nightmare
nightlong. Chinese
rose! Chinese rose! Tell me
where did I lose
my happiness

Songs spin on my forehead
Deep beauty! Gold claws
throw life into the abyss of pain
My love opens in brief summer
like injured feelings in final
battle with the death of land
Rose! Chinese rose! Roses
burst in my chest. Tell me
when will those who begin to understand
remember me in delirium
and forgive the dying

DRAWBRIDGE
  [van Gogh: "The Langlois Bridge," 1888]

Bright pure water
one side of the ferry hidden in reeds
The boatman's hand brushes catkins
magpie calls from the corolla
A sunny day. Birds shiver
Young women gather at the riverside
their wash-sticks like flower stems
unfolding on the smooth stones
The river ambles
Bristly thistles drowse day long
pheasants scout out their house
and stick tail-feathers in the donkey's bells

Who's in there chewing olive leaves
lying in the dark shade of the cypress' belly
Eyes that are covered by water chestnuts
chat with summer as it sports in the river water
Blue quivers in a cat's eyes
Noon expands the exquisite silk
Who's in there, pale of face, biting the roots of reeds
agape at the delicate frame of the distant drawbridge
A carriage ticks in the sun's pendulum
Trembling, he presses his heart
too overcome to speak a word
facing the boundless peace and silence

Holy day of sun
the present of grape juice from your lover
Your heart leaps with a string nailed in memory
The lotuses in a music reach out, hands under the field
to smooth away the pain of your life
give you calm and let you lie at ease
on the open wing of a dahlia
Cruel! Brief happy time

SCENE
[van Gogh: "The Plain with Farm Near Auvers," 1890]

Plants ripen, their round
mouths draw water from the soil. Their
slim waists sway before barn doors
Seeds sing in tiny gowns
Fields stretch, like ponies, their shining hair
spread across the land

Who has heard the fall of
food on the rock? Children
play in the farmer's hand
A poet wakes up. He sits on the roots of a
yellow tung tree. The roots grow into his flesh
His face glows with the happiness of a plant
Houses at a distance bathe in the fields
Red pine glitter from bright rifts in the clouds
Land! you are innocent and boundlessly deep

Who weeps behind earth
refusing to give his heart
The heart is ripe, fragrant
Wheat leaps in the stomachs of cows
My brother! in your throat
sings the priceless diamond of memory
A mare gives birth to six colts. Walnuts
carom from their hooves into
the bell of the noon sun's trumpet
Who, this moment, nestles
roughened chest flat against the
lonely earth, crying with muffled sobs

SUNFLOWER
[van Gogh: "Sunflowers," 1888]

Sunflower claws walk the earth
across starving stones
A light, a call
a face full of seeds
shouting to get nearer the sun
The face unfolds in pain
proud tolerance
A sharp flame
burns at the sun's throat

Sun! I feel from beneath my feet
your rising power
and your madness
penetrating my skull! A bright drill
cuts open my skin
A hundred of my hot-tempered hearts
    rush towards you
life upright on the wings of a giant beast
cutting the dark
    with a wheel of light

Here is your palace
Oleander, pomegranate, cypress
in a throng of gray mice
alive and satisfied
Stags sparkle. In the pain of struggle
I'm granted a
favor and my life is established
on the land extolled by
those I love. My head held high
to hold the sun
    before I break

Yellow! color of dreams
Light with a rolling tongue
takes over my words and my pulse
Sky fortissimo among opening sunflowers
Life! sun where my father lives secluded
Flame! surrounding me
beholding my glory
burning me suddenly from inside
My heart, contorted in chasing you
sings furiously, shackled in blood

TONIGHT
   [van Gogh: "Starry Night over the Rhône," 1888]

Rock, September! A dark-skinned child
lights the lamp in the tower
Its golden orange shines at the moon
Rock, September! Tap on your water jar
in the evening breeze

My days are filled with secrets
But when? Can I make those I
love understand my wishes
by describing the chrysanthemum's pistil
My brow is covered with candles
Trumpets bend towards happiness
trumpeting my joy
to the peaceable Rhône

Love me! the Rhône where antlers
disappear. Stars shine out above me
Songs from happy lips
as this wine jar of tonight's sky
tilts towards my delight
Love me, September! Rock
Rock me with tripod feet
Shake me with the warm charm of your glaze
The dark-skinned boy is going home to the river
Tonight, my heart, here
you will feel no pain, no loneliness

STARRY NIGHT
   [van Gogh: "The Starry Night," 1889]

Evening is a trembling amber
People, tiny insects
curl up in the horseshoe-shaped air
Language calls out in the dark
Who is it races the fear in our souls
to describe the distant light
to open the constellations, flames licking the sky
With a strength that crosses village and cypress
I call out to Nature: I'm in pain

Brother, give me your hand
Two animal claws will come to grips
My poem, the roaring of wounded animals
The sky's giant teeth gleam over mountaintops exposed
Love is at war, a bird flies high
and changes his feathers as the river suddenly divides
Ah, what kind of drum
will stretch your skin and mine
Blood flows through evening sand
Our creativity is the drummer
grimly tapping out our hearts
In the deserted night
we hear them howling at our dream of life

PORTRAIT
  [van Gogh: "Self-Portrait," 1889]

Say, who can grasp pain with its whirlpool claw
its boiling sulphur. My eyes quake in acid
That heart, in the place you despise, tortures you
after you're safely home

Across a suffering sea. Defeated sails
sag over water lying like a marble slab
Tormented ships tremble
their souls adrift
Cries for help harden
in the smile on every survivor's face

I hang my head and sob
Your face sparkles in my night-long pain
The eyes of a she-wolf who has lost her children
a narwhal writhing on the rocks
watching its own blood stain the ocean

Pain. Human to shrew in a single day
My bones go up in flames
Their marrow becomes condiment
O my soul, like a hurricane
every impure evening, they
pull down the empty house in your
always troubled outlook

Art, bridging ideograms, sees where life
comes from. The land is shaking. I treasure
the pearls in my heart, presented, evenings, in
salt, to the traveler

BLUES
   [van Gogh: "The Night Café," 1888]

The hand stirring coffee
in obscure night
tugs at the shirt of some passerby
Light is like a moth
fluttering. In the berry's pit
the claw of the beast moves
Before sleeping he pours blood
down his raw throat
Night, I hear you bawl into the mike
"Not a thing in the world to do—drop
your drawers, baby"

Human beings sit on chairs
tread on plants, looking stern
Clocks tick off numbers of insulted souls
The mike in the neck sings madly out
"Dark heart, dark night and my
lover, the well-known card-sharp"
Homeless. Loiterers
scratch their faces, echo the song

Derelict! displays animal skin in the warm
night, showing off magnificent houses
Pines tremble in the shiver of souls
beasts pass in mobs, not daring to look back
I feel fear on distant lands
Seed is buried all about me

The waiter faces me, eyes at a loss
A man out cold hangs on to a shark's fin
navigating a caffeine fantasy
The coffee shop sings hoarsely in my ear
Babies cry their unfortunate destinies

Ancestors panic in the very stones
Shall we simply throw this land away
Artists: sad and poor, you have
only poetry, bright sunlight
the music that turns people inward
to themselves! Nothing else to cling to

REMEMBERING

Words! before you led me to destruction
the guava seed was a clean hand
prodding me to get on my way
I've torn the skins of things, like crushing grapes
My heart spread its wings
hovered in the round heart of the wine
Men's faces, then, stood in oil
Had I ever used the word *detest?*

My mouth is a horse's mouth
—language my hay, dried in sun and air
The feet of birds are buried under the hay
lizards on one side building a nest
Talking about them causes me an
animal pain that pierces my heart
takes my hand, places it on the word
to find the spot from which feelers sprout

Childhood! My poems a clean house
the fields a ball rolling
Mother's two baskets on a pole across her shoulder
Over emerald leaves, rivers rush on
Had I ever worn the anxious look I wear now?
Make my poems a rag to wipe with—wash here, wash there
Make grating sounds—wrench here, wrench there
Throw the books on the floor
From a snowy sky remote from humanity
snowflakes striking become soundless tears
Had I ever tried to praise beauty?
My entire body glittering quicksilver
my first song was in my youth
My teeth shone then like the horns of a fawn
in the pride of life, my smile unhidden

I walked then
like water drawn from a well

Remembering! this conch shell
Golden yellow makes me see
the flesh that quivers within life
Sound of stones contracting
The sound of fleshWaves washing over strands of sinew
The drowned become shells
and in my breathing speak their understanding
of a world that follows after death
Vengeance on the living, through silent sounds
Remember! trees felled and dry and rotten
Ants on a stump
crawling in a ring
Light encircles you
People—in moving forward, they fall
into the deepest dark. The most
radical among them try hardest to look out
drawing nearer, day by day, unfeeling flesh
Seeking that conch
we are still children
laughing at the sky

Words! before you lead me to destruction
I want to see clearly your real shape
Living among people, I am
a wolf, not yet grown into exile
avoiding the traps of words, of phrases
All around me, throats steeped in venom
swaying in the barrens! The four seasons
hide within men's eyes
revealing the spots of the leopard
My heart, how can you not press your lips
to patches of sunlight in the mud?
How can you not wail for an animal?

An infant rises before me
flexes four limbs, weeps
Earth glitters, not yet fouled by men
Then how can I not sing?
One after another my poems
make the sound of chains shaken
one of my legs crushed by the crowd
my cry of indignation and despair

Crack the world to its core, you'll find a poem
Standing in the presence of poetry
is all that can make my whole body tremble
Hearing insects make love
my blood gushes from poetry's heart
words tumbling over each other
clambering over light-beams in the grain
Empty conch shell. Anxiety and respect
together forge a brain. Still in a woman's womb
love, gleaming gold from head to foot, rising
on this fluid, a hand takes hold of the ocean's horn
From the moment a melody called to me
life showed me the delicate bones of men
filled with a marrow of purest gold and
praised by poetry
Our ancestors appreciated in silence
the sharp shards of those bones
the trembling of these healthy beasts
at life's very center
Fields of flowers opened by light

My heart! Could you then pronounce
from your precious lips the filthy
word *detest?*

II

FIRST LOVE

Calling ceaselessly your name
in order to feel how I was caught and
plunged into birth
I cried, meaning to refuse the un-
welcoming world
Pain contains me
frightened and confused
calling your name
Nightmare clutches me
My heart is torn by hungry
wolves within my flesh

First love, like a mirror
broken. Pain
of my birth, life's
pain. Love leads me by the nose
I'm in a hard grip
pulled along. Wolves
prowl in all directions

SITTING IN THE SUN

Sitting in the sun, he writes
and turns the darkness in his heart
to the light
In the sun he is
surprised to see himself
That enemy, who stuffs your gut and holds your
soul by force, ages you
Unspeakable fear
takes hold. Sometimes for no good reason you
hate yourself. That enemy
inside you
gets off a good exit line
while you doze in the sun

Sitting in the sun, he dreams
and turns
life inside out. This way we can
live again, distinguish the
too soiled facets. We were young then and
careless. Thread hung
from torn parts. We didn't know how
to use our bodies properly
Only sitting in the sun we
begin to know love
Just as we begin to feel warm and enlightened
death—like time malfunctioning
—stumbles out from a living short cut
with a good poem

Sitting in the sun:
the light is leading him
off from where he's been
sleeping away his life

DREAM

They stand up, go away
expose one side of their bodies
outside my sleep
They saunter side by side
while I'm by myself
asleep between layers of the dark
See how relaxed
they are
coming in and out of
the spots I detest
They clomp over and
trample on me. They spread
four-fingered hands
and pinch their shanks
then throw themselves down neatly
with no sound at all
To hear distinctly
under the dark
the meeting of man and dream
people screaming, breath
caught in terror

They get up. They disappear
Reappear. Approaching the
absolute, nights let down their
hair to victims of insomnia
Dreams are dark. Far
off from life
I turn and toss in
darkness. I'm pulling
the blanket up. I'm
pulling it enough
to cover up my head

INTERPLAY

The living
are shadows of the dead
They make noise
When the dead dream in the silent dark
when the dead wake
the living feel sudden terror
day-long loneliness
It is the dead
who have left home
to meet their family on the way
The living, day by day, age
It is the dead who try to
return to the world
The living feel alone
when they meet each other
They shout "Who
loves me?"
It is the dead standing
next to them
The dead clench their teeth
with contempt
with revenge
Because the living
are always giving the dead a bad name

ZONE

There's water there, the garden opens
Singing, you wear your red skirt
Summer is a pattern of
flowers on your sash
Days pass
as you turn. Birds
fold their wings ten thousand ways
All this time I'm far from home
Along the road, wheat fields breathe from
their broad lungs, the land
sends out clear noises. All this
time, I'm trying to get across it
Soil circles earth
I've a thousand expressions
to display my yellow face
Wheat fields hum a song
          —in the East

There's steel. Highways
cut through what used to be fields
Jazz bleats
in the shadow of high buildings
There, the homeless
find wheat fields in their dreams
At the blast of ten trumpets a new
continent arises and the sea
rolls the passion of sex. In the East
the voice of home
breaks up each day. I cover my face
sobbing among ruins
Still I try to track
the zone I dream of. On my way
seeing my youth, seeing

51

middle age mounting me
like two sharp and
shiny rib bones
hampering my breath
here on western land
I find that any direction I
walk, every impulse whatever
points clearly, unambiguously
        towards—China

RESPECT

Only for you, my heart
I maintain my ardent love
despairing of humankind
For you I keep the fire lit
You come out of darkness and thought
You feel how life is still warm
You light all the lamps, try
talking with human beings
only to find them simple-minded, ignorant
their hands occupied with life's trifles
When you escape that stuffy house
things of beauty gleam
gently in the sun
so clean
In my life, only
you, my heart, move across
other lives, follow me, my bosom friend
After the rain, after
some talk with other
souls refreshed by books, could we not
go for a walk, watch
daylight glide across tree trunks
animals stretch their limbs
and pass us nimbly by. Birds
cry out in nightmare
Little by little
the sun in serenity in-
vades the space that night vacates
Maybe after a long walk
we'll come back, the fields with us
The grasses will announce
"After this rain
comes harvest"

HOMING

As I walk homeward
dusk surrounding
in groups behind me wanderers
sing out their songs of labor
carrying their hands as they would carry money
carefree, never asking where they're headed
Since I left youth behind
I see my days each day in strangers. Once I
sang from waywardness
happy in my passion. Each day
a line of poetry. For all the things
I seek and for those I curse

As I step onto that road
that cuts empty and still through overgrowth
rivers glitter around me
The world I entered once and wasted
sways in my heart with a gentle sweetness
I touch the soil in quiet ecstasy
Things crowd around me
each singing in its bound
For the first time, I hold my head up
In that light I need no language
to express my gratitude
Youth has fully ripened, as fruit
bodies out between pit and skin
my poems press out around my heart
simple and full of feeling
holding the dreams and the labor
of a life of pain

As I walk this plain of consciousness
in a fullness of light
where every object vanishes
reappears, metamorphoses
I feel "home"
inside my body
and these pains and aspirations
though together in one
dwelling, belong to different centuries and
different lives. Home gleams in my
blood. My blood
flows round the house which is
made of light. My bounding heart
beats in cadence with
this house radiating its
pure white beams

THE YOUNG BELIEVER

All life long he sings one song
God pulls up a chair
holds meditation in your heart
God says, now every day, three hundred sixty-five
in a year, I think of
what I've gone and done
Children, you don't use your heads, you
just sing. Song
is a meander, one end
hooked up to the soul

Three hundred sixty-five days a year
And every day, as God gets to thinking
you start in singing
As names for the newly dead
are raised from the ground
hunger fills bodies in one crowd
and in another crowd, the way
crocodiles clan in a group, slide
back into water from the shore. Hatred
like wheat which ripens twice a year
springs up from the scene of human life, is
turned into bread and
wine for celebration
Every day the gods put their heads together
and try to figure out where they
went wrong in managing humanity, how they
bungled their "god-like erect"
Children, only you
can turn your eyes from this world
in order to gaze into your own souls
standing in wretched weather ruined
by endless mortal bitching

Children, you sing
to turn yourselves into music
and blend with the scarce sunbeams

Every day, you try to sing to its end
the song unending until your life ends
When you begin to sing, the gods
are out of business
You pick up the work the
gods botched—and go on with it
You turn the wine, the bread back into wheat
In songs and verses
old people, women in travail
watch shoots spring up
in the heart's furrows
The heart becomes the soil most
intimately human. We put our
children, our lovers into
the soil. We come from dust and to dust
return, singing with our wounded feelings
We're starting to sing again, after an
epoch of dudgeon. To get to this level
has taken a lifetime

BACK

That's not the place for you, father
Snakes, there, raise their bodies up
as the young do while making love
Every night, there, down in the valley
crowds of repentant people gather
The rocks at the foot of the valley
roar at blocks of sky the darkness
covers. Father, that's
not the place for you
Your sight is swollen
Birds sleep lethargically behind
dawn's gigantic curtain

On bankrupt sidewalks
American kids
talk about a just
war in the desert
Smoke thick and spreading blooms like
oriental blossoms. Truth marches out in steel
In the pit their claws have dug
the sum of things stops changing
Father, that's no place for you
There's a center anywhere
Filled with misgiving, you find
all around you: the homeless rich

You still need to go back
to the East, to your simple but
quite warm home
That's where old folk belong
there where the young
rush to get out, still asleep
Sky there is sky
and will never mean anything else
People there live
satisfied lives

EARTH

Dry eyed, we gaze down the road
at parents and children returning: scattered
bones abandoned on the waste land of memory
Each and every night the dead come back
carrying bouquets, wearing laundry-marked shirts
recognizing the sleepers. They guard us
When they leave, they leave their bouquets
next to our pillows. We wake, see the sunlight
Maybe we hear birds. Awake, we've
first of all the palpable recollection
of having been somewhere, having felt some
cold, having done something. Wide
awake: to wake is to forget
What shines is only the morning sun
and its light is not from life

Our eyes dry, an earth remote from us
eats, drinks, sickens us
bewitches and crazes us. Still
deeply in love, we
left our lovers. Leaving our
childhood there, we left our roots
Only in sleep do we
rejoin our relations. Each night
returning, quietly to feel
all old familiar faces, before
dawn, before we wake
Since then, living between two realities
we age at double speed
sunk in a confusion of
everyday and inner worlds
We live and move along widening fissures
of fatigue, despair, dream, forgetfulness

Childhood remains on that earth
of no return. Sleeping
we make love to old lovers
loving again in sleep, kissing and
drinking that earth in on our lover's body
weeping for past love, writing for
love past, waking, wanting
to sleep again. Sitting in the sun, I
watch myself age towards that distant earth
aching to lift the light and the fruit that
loom in the loneliness, lifting them high
in the old love, here among untold strangers

DRUG

Waking one summer
morning in New England, I
remembered the breasts of the girl in my dream
My hands still with the feel
of clutching the round subway strap
I stand still. Life moves on
Her eyes remind me of an owl
In the darkness, my love for her
crawls quietly through weed-filled fields
The owl dives noiselessly
Her mouth holds my tongue
Long hairy legs clamp
tight—my cry of horror
explodes in the moment of love

This is the drug I imbibe each day
a woman I love madly
Her skin is whiter than mine
She has grace, elegance. Her
fingers caress my
skin always with tenderness
But nightmares come
when love is deepest
Their memory whips my face
pushes me seven different directions
then pieces me back together
and sends me loving
in the constant, violent dreams
of my sweaty bed
Loving, hard work which
rejoices my spirit, tires and confuses my
body—I realize I'm addicted

Such is life in the New England summer
Violence, love, terror. When I open my mouth
my tongue, that's used to tasting words
tastes a pair of small breasts
I feel poetry and the drug
all mixed together. They
boil and bubble in
the seven celestial areas of my body
I move on—my life stands still. I
love that woman, such grace, such elegance
She teaches me to give up poetry
She teaches me, in her flesh, in my
fatigue and loss, in such
desperate loneliness and
in her love full of terror and hysteria
suddenly to see and to understand
the truth of myself and also
of the thing I'm so deeply addicted to

WHITE RUBBER MASK

I hold up this face. It looks out of
two eyes, with a wide open mouth
Now it brings to mind the Hopi
diminished after thirteen centuries
In one of their innumerable mystic rites
all the Hopi opened wide their mouths
to shout—but no sound came
I'm waking from sleep
Why is it so dark
in that wide open mouth? In that
screaming silent mouth I see always
death chasing death. I see death
crushing underfoot the teeth of creatures
Death never makes a sound. Death
merely appears, like that open mouth
The shout must come from us. Crowds vanish

Will my perplexities be resolved? My
thoughts trip up my feet and
haul me into greater horrors
Am I in a dream or on New Mexican mesa
I see the white rubber mask
human cries transmuted to "energy"
Matter still exists. It opens its
round mouth wide. Generation after
generation does battle and sinks
slowly out of sight invoking gods and spirits
Death's mouth is forced open
to let such desires and such travail
burst out—tragic, indignant, injured
This is the pueblo where the Indians live
Rivers have dried up. Dust drifts from
here to there. In my sleep

I hold up this white rubber mask
Three black holes confront me
It laughs. The rubber is thick
a hard and springy substance
I know already, before waking
I will wake in terror

FORGIVE

Hatred I need no longer to
learn or to erase from my experience in this life
gaining though it is among the new generation
I feel the century change, grasped
by dessicated claws of that crowd of old men who, exiled by
their century, try to carry the century into exile with them
I stand between crabbed youth and age. As if crossing a bridge
I move along this pestilential century
I know exactly what I'm doing
When I stop thinking, stop writing, when I stare
at crowds on both sides of the bridge and beneath its arches
I hear them railing against me
They curl under the weight of their own self-oppression
Sperm spurts from their tongues
When I stop writing
I know they are part of the century's sickness
excited by hatred, by self-abuse
They're spunky and they get to the top
Some of them pass themselves off as poets
and devote their whole day drawing
    doodles of their cocks

I've more important things to do in this life
I need to study, to listen for the soul's instruction
amid jeering crowds and unjust treatment
to lift life to a cleaner higher level
I'm crossing the bridge that leads to the ultimate
watching this new breed's viral growth
witnessing violence and poverty—hatred like a mother
carries those twins. The old eventually
chuck their hopes while the young
go on cheering. Material desires
thrust up like a totem for our century

My life is to be lonely and to write
and to engage my soul in pondering
Out my window: polluted rain on spoiled landscape and
the bawling of a coming generation just squeezing
through the narrow gate of carnal desire to be
plopped on the operating table
Crimes are the lessons we've to learn in
this life. See the present century
hectic from head to toe, delirious with fever
lost in new litters of humanity
Floods of people, flowing through long years
the century's purulence. With hatred
with ignorance, a passion for self-abuse and
excelling imagination, they join in history's
crime and degradation. They're alive and
well. In the process of human awakening and
purification, evil
is what we have to take into account

FACES

When you stop thinking and trembling
your face like a piece of
cowhide scorching curls inward. Time
like mice runs through the ceiling beam. You
hear its quick and cautious scurrying. Your face
grows older in the silence. Inside your
body, you feel something quick and cautious
running through
A feeling like cowhide
curling inward slowly as it burns
light suspended along with
the curvature of things
In the surrounding dark and my
body's peace, I watch human
faces curled outward by a hundred years
peel like the bark from tree trunks
dessicated and resin-parched. Human faces
twisted and lost, peel away from the spirit
Violence creates a quiet in existence, fear
curved layer by layer into the heart of silence
Something quick and
cautious runs through human memory
bearing traces of burning, the grief
of things gone

So you feel when you stop
thinking and trembling. Morning late
you lie on your bed. Sun crosses your pillow
inch by inch. The room grows brighter
You're hearing the cry of things
irrevocably twisted

A SNAKE WITH EXPERIENCE

From yon to hither
through the mud they slide
their glistening bellies. Heads
hoisted at anything in their way

Power of darkness
when they come erect
dropping down directly
Whereas the light from
sacrifice, the patience
from truth—these ascend

THE SHAME OF FLESH

When I lose the will to win
I find the crowd turning away with
flabby hands, slabs of flesh which
moments ago, were wringing and
pounding each other. Honor
is like an animal quartered
Now a holiday, audience in
circulation. Silence as the artists exit
Behind the crowd, lonely
days, mob faced with pain
and fantasy. Enthusiasm
outlasts contempt. After I
lose the will to win
it all comes back
In peace, I've finally
peace

Don't trust the singing voice
Too many echoes gather
mixed with the crowd's murmurs
the smell of flesh and fancy
designer clothes. Can the singer
hear pure singing in his body
filled with the desire to sing
in tune only with his inner life
The pure sound calls
from within, touching perhaps
only the soul and not
those surrounding fabrics
not the flesh trembling
in its shame

I see peace in
peace, feeling it come
from the heart's deep
glory. Can you turn away from
the imagined honor
Before the audience
walk away. Before
the agony of shame
Before all desires of the
flesh burst

BIOGRAPHY

Against darkness the shiny pelt
slides down. Night
chews the bones of tiny creatures
I try to see into the
past that pain has pressed shut
The white woman
watches me in her happiness
She doesn't understand how
I am full of anger, how
an armed government
can modify the soul
within a body
Ah but the only indestructible
is flesh. It can
bend serenely in the dark while
the humiliated soul flees screaming

To squat at the root
of animality. Their sex
flickers in my brain
Something I must have
felt this dark night. My two
little fingers twist and
pinch the lips spitting out
the word "motherland." Motherland
source of my destitute wandering
abroad, in
shame. Against darkness
the shiny pelt. I weep for
love of the white woman. Pure love
Sublime love. I hate
my hysterical past

Who can stop him? Facing the
way he came, hateful and contemptuous
he turns humiliated and keeps on
walking. The night maintains
my body temperature. He wakes
from his long anger. Who can force him
back to it, whether
abroad or in his motherland
When the soul returns
existence is ratified
Flesh is weak but
strong if you feel the soul
Light shines out like matter
lifting you in clarity
You stand in the road and weep
weeping the fullness of love
and the only thing that can stop
you, finally
stop you, is
there are limits to
what a body can do

NOCTURNE ON A NEW THEME

One after another, westward
we drive "love"—this
fashionable car. Its bumper
cuts through cheers and catcalls
Love cuts open our bodies. We
live in a strange country
Love between white and Asian
is a complicated
soup. N.B.: the white
drink soup as an appetizer
while to the Asian, soup means
end of banquet

To make love or to leave
whites like to shout at the
top of their lungs. The yellow
manage with a look. One after another
moving in the flesh. Only in bed
are humans allowed to air their
hate without reserve. Biting
cursing, backbiting—all
indicate succulent loving

Westward our love moves, on
four tires with a slow leak
Every night through the
pain of growth. Like a whacked nail
bent, we're making love. The love we've
made breaks through the gulf between
races—a work completed
in the dark. The flesh
shines. We know
who we are. Where
are we

STEPS IN THE DARK

The door is locked
Raw iron on iron to enclose the
dark in its cold darkness
Last step as the stairway
ends. I mount
the hanging ladder, away from
fearful and painful dreams

I climb
Every day of my life
I hear screeches
Darkness gathers in
dimming light
The power of growth
forces all the doors
A man with a strange face
strolls through my life
steps on me, his
short legs kicking each other
in my brain. Of late
my life diminishes. I hear
the screeches
Nothing surfaces

along life stretched taut
All the open doors
locked. From the bottom rung I
climb stubbornly towards
the top. All the tightly locked
doors, open

HESITATING MAN

Because I'm far from
youth's last impulse to failure
that impulse has hurried me into middle age
Or because, too far from home
the dry land of my land and
continuous dreaming homewards
has turned me waking
weird, wits wandering. Is it
real when I feel the pain
of middle aged exile? Or
is it dream-pain? We're always
aware what we need. Not money
but an abstract something
Nation. Spirit. To
die for a belief. To kill

Pain is like
bleeding flesh, abscess
It grows in periods of calm
close bound up with the bones
There's nothing I believe in. Always
impulsive, I doubt myself, would
like to be far from myself
with careful application doing
harm to myself
Helplessness. The pain of living
far from my homeland and middle aged
lets me sometimes forget myself
and write something surprising
broad along the vast background

ANNIVERSARY

To see the fruit, from the roots, in a
strange place. Something
disappears, is lost. An anniversary's
inevitable quarreling. People crowd in
around the roots. The ground shifts from
under my legs, leaving the genitals
between two mirrored days
Passion ruins my face
directly, not via the sexual organs
I see fruit. A fantastic sense of
happiness lost

This is the price one pays, the price
of having parents. They grow old, their
children living unhappily in an
alien place. Return is another
kind of unhappiness
The country is old, we
think of leaving as soon as possible. Those
who have left feel the pain of "away"
It's all tied in with souls. We don't
know. One year, another year: like
the two sides of a coin. Recognize it and
act accordingly. Something
is lost

Anniversary: wrangling always with
myself, who would believe it? We still
try to live closer to the roots
The wanderer has no message. Nothing but
distance. On those same aging
faces, you will see
happiness and unhappiness

CROSSED REALITIES

When I've lain quietly three
hours, snow begins to fall
Patiently, snow whitens this
dark January. In the damp night
I encounter a friend I haven't seen for
ten years. The bulge of a muscle
took his life. How did he return? So
radiant. Let me touch him: his body's
warm and soft. When I lie down in quiet
before snow has begun to fall
I hear the old chairs creak
and the pens on my desk roll. The
sky out the window is like my mistress's
ardent sex, daunting. I see the playground
where I used to hang out as a child

The ex-owners of this room
appear in a thin light. Old Acquaintances
on first meeting. My
mistress comforts me hysterically
When I call on love for help, she
screams in terror. I struggle
through a long sleep
refusing the plummet into deeper
sleep. My old friend's body is
warm, soft. Furniture is moving about with
exaggerated tumult. I've never
seen so clearly just
where I am. In the silent house of
snow, I see myself in
return
without a trace

THE PASSAGE TO HEAVEN

I see him from a distance. Sleep
is a long narrow train with
many empty seats. I see myself
sitting, traveling somewhere
Along the way, on my left
I see unfold, meticulously, a
mysterious orange and ochre scape. I
almost wake up
Heaven is just back of my
eyes, almost as if—the train moving
just a bit faster or
stopping—I might become
the first person to see heaven
and return. I can't tell you
how that passage
woke me at midnight and made
me happy. The train reaches its
destination in the tropics. I'm
waking slowly and longing for
two women I love

TURN INWARD, INWARD

I discovered one day that
love is my life's
disease, rooted
in my childhood like
seeds sown too early. Well
intended, but seeds can't
penetrate frost and
ruined lonely
childhood. When I
try to love, I find I'm
hating. There's nothing
worth our fear but love, but
hatred itself

The question isn't to be or
not to be. Wherever we go we
spread our disease. It's a question
of being conscious or unconscious
If I hadn't tried to love, things
would be better and I wouldn't
hate myself like this
I slap my own face and
see clearly the
sickness of living

Daylong I see this face
aging, ever
uglier. I see hatred, how its root
digs into the flesh. I pretend
to glow with health, my very
life an illness. When I
sleep my covers are
shit. Sleep is a
latrine, my body

a plank across it. Waking
is to walk that plank, watching
the filth beneath my feet, the
worms at work. I think I
see my former life
I see my inward shape

I shame my mother's
womb, brighter and warmer
than this cess-pit. Love
never came there. Now there's
only a plank across. Here
is the root of my disease
My love's lower
part is all I
love and worship. Only there
I let my life
pass by with care and
in awe. I hate her
brain, her thought

I love her shining eyes
her body full of love, the way
she calls out *Fuck me!* My body
fills with inspiration
I feel this life
erect, loving in
hate, hating in love, the
hard adult body in a re-
turn to childhood. Or else I'm
just a dream. Real
life I recognize: the latrine

One day I discovered that being
loved makes love
dissipate, makes us desperate

LOVE

Can't you learn love
through forgetting, understand love
by relaxing. That's what you need
when the body looks like rained-on snow
as footprints
run away in haste
even while it's winter
Can you understand the rage
of repressed anger—it comes from love
and, in love's name and the name of
courage, it ruins love. When the heart
is more eager for intimacy than the body
the most dangerous moment has arrived

Desperate moment. Love becomes more concrete
than genitals—and more dangerous
Love is an army gone loco, a child
sunk in humiliation. Love is
everything you ever want, everything you
can't get in this life. You ask from love every-
thing you know anything about and it's all
dangerous. You know how to begin
but not how to stop. In the name of
love, you lay waste your life

Love is the soul's inner energy. If un-
stopped altogether, it may become
hate, and then you're lost. As long as body
is more eager for intimacy than is heart, it's
dark but you can see the exit sign
Long love and strong desire
win love. Then standing

high in the dark. From there one can trace
the course of our lives, marked
by pain and injustice

             You. You, and
we also. Love is just the beginning of
soul's maturing. Soul may need several
bodily destructions. Body's torment
doesn't become soul's, but remains in the body's
suffering. Who understands this
stands high in the dark and
can see the exit
               up there

LOVE IN DIFFICULTY

Reconciled
I feel close to the source
I am rocked in the long ark of
poetry. In another reality my hand
writes lines with the odor of plants
My body, in its difficult
times, enjoys them—keeping life
aware and
closer to the source. Pleasure without
self-consciousness. Life is a trembling
liquid, sending out strains of
unprompted praise
The ark of poetry
glides away and along
on this clear rippling
water
People love and feel loved, feel
happiness calm and pure

Love in difficulty is my
poem. One stanza is complete. In another
reality, a new stanza is being
born, but isn't yet there
I grope for lost arrivals
Life, through me, falls
weeping. Can't you feel the difficulty
of connecting the first line
with a whole life? The hardship of
this life makes life, in another
reality, glide
Much love turns us, vertiginous, takes
away suffering. The ark of poetry, at last
watertight, rises in the latest

days of this life. Water to
water. Water lifts water
in the clear calm of poetry
In my love's fullness I
bless those who still
have many lives to live

MARCH

March fades. Like
a traveler, the farther he goes
the more he regrets his life
We weep day long
for the crowd on their way
Too close, empty rooms of flesh
tremble, souls howl within
demanding hard shells
for keeping their distance. At night
sensitive people write, without speaking
Confused people make love, working hard
to feel something outside their bodies
But you, you weep all night, cavernous room
of empty flesh. Rueful
echoes. Women, I
love you. In the wet snow of March
you walk farther and farther, imagining
safety and security for the flesh
In this life, keep some distance
between you and your soul

If I could only not use my body
In the feeling of worship to
experience the soul's growing
its interaction with the
aging body. As when I write, I
talk with my many past lives
unconscious love-travel, making
love. When the body's
tired, I feel its glow
embarrassed in return. I
know how to cry, to shout
to complain. With the woman lost

we cross the fury of love
March fades. Souls crying
bring unnumbered storms
rolling to this over-
crowded dirtying
planet

THE SKIN OF LOVE

To learn love in
loneliness and to feel
hatred is a root sunk the
other side of darkness. On
either side is life and death
When we're happy, we
stop questioning
and we call that state *love*

From the bottom of the dark, to
live upwards, approaching
unknowing. To weep. Consciousness
void of reason. That state
we call *waking*. Like a
bridge from abyss to abyss, from
void to void, the gist is
all our effort every
moment of our lives. A love
falters, see: another love grows
Love in confusion. Between
death and death there is
one lamp and one only

To love in loneliness
desperate effort
exhausting way of life
far from my own country, returning
only in dreams
Country means to me
a plane of light
a way of living I
must, and heartily, accept
The return of desire is

a calloused skin, both
sides of which strive
to know life, living
and death, dying

RAINY DAY

Life's desires
concrete and clear
in mid-life anxiety
like a fall of
uneasy waters
Childhood is a hollow
among the rocks
Four remembered horses
galloping the bank
Those who watch those limbs in
motion report *horses running*
Their shanks remind me of
the look in my lover's
eyes when she's relaxed and happy
The pressure of mid-life is
there from birth and runs the years
as horses run the riverbank
crossing the light of time
A violent force inwards
In a single moment, bearing the
burden of life entire, they
leap, they feel the burden
easy—with joy, with satisfaction
seeing how beauty
gathers at the center, solid
Or collapsing overburdened. Or
falling into ordinary mid-life
excess of energy without release

NOSTALGIA

A man looks back on the land as it
rises. He sees youth as
nails hammered into the dust. Motherland
is the land he can't take with him
Parents distant, decrepit. Wall
collapsing. Home is a
hunk of meat on a hook
Childhood a butcher knife raised, wooden handle
decaying memory. A man
looks forward to the land as it rises
the hollows running primly
As the stranger turns his head, herds
of animals are mating. The man
lonely, nostalgic
hears screams, and again
rising from below, screams

BEFORE THE GOOD WEATHER

Be lonely
be sleepless

Crying deep in the night
look: a century ago

a woman loved art
its endurance

That love-sickness went deep into her heart
a faltering life-shaking love

A hundred years later: these
carefully arranged words

perpetuate love
a spring of living water

A youthful heart, in-
somniac, is struck by ancient

loneliness. I come to a halt
look around, then gaze at myself

Tears flow unwittingly. To
know life

is to be forgotten by
those I value, to be passed by

Once, in deep night, my
tears flowed without warning

for this life I lead
on my own, alone

Proudly alone, in a
foreign land, I write

until sleep overcomes me

This book was computer typeset in 10 pt. Palatino and designed by Rosmarie Waldrop. It was printed on 55 lb. Writers' Natural (an acidfree paper), smyth-sewn and glued into paper covers by McNaughton & Gunnn in Saline, Michigan. There are 1000 copies.